For my folks, who told me about the Tinsleys, and others; for three Michaels and two Mikes; for Pedr; for Alan; and mostly, for Chris.

Mike Stott

FUNNY PECULIAR

AMBER LANE PRESS

First published in 1978
by Amber Lane Productions Limited,
Amber Lane Farmhouse,
The Slack, Ashover,
Derbyshire S45 0EB

Printed in Great Britain.

ISBN 0 906399 02 5

Funny Peculiar was first produced at the Schauspielhaus, Bochum, in 1974. Its first English production was given at the Liverpool Everyman on 30 January, 1975, directed by Alan Dossor and with the following cast:

TREVOR TINSLEY	Nicholas le Prevost
IRENE TINSLEY	Julie Walters
REV A. J. THWAITE	David Peart
SGT HARRY ASQUITH	Nick Stringer
MRS BALDRY	Eileen O'Brien
STANLEY BALDRY	Matthew Kelly
SHIRLEY SMITH	Katherine Fahy
ERIC SMITH	Bill Nighy
DESMOND AINSLEY	Kevin Lloyd
SHANE PRITCHARD	David Peart

Funny Peculiar opened in London at the Mermaid Theatre on 22 January, 1976 with Richard Beckinsale as Trevor and Julie Walters as Irene.

AMBER LANE PLAYS
Series Editor: Judith Scott

Also available in this series:

Whose Life is it Anyway?
Brian Clark

Once A Catholic
Mary O'Malley

For information on these and forthcoming titles write to:
Amber Lane Press, Amber Lane Farmhouse,
The Slack, Ashover, Derbyshire S45 0EB

FUNNY PECULIAR

Characters

TREVOR TINSLEY
IRENE TINSLEY
REV A. J. THWAITE
SGT HARRY ASQUITH
MRS BALDRY
STANLEY BALDRY
SHIRLEY SMITH
ERIC SMITH
DESMOND AINSLEY
SHANE PRITCHARD

The action takes place in a village somewhere in the Pennines.

FUNNY PECULIAR

A pub.

[*Pre-set fades to a BLACKOUT. SOUND ONLY.*]

ONE: You must be joking. They weren't.

TWO: They were. They were.

ONE: Oh, surely not.

TWO: I'm telling you, aren't I? They were . . . you know. Hard at it.

ONE: But he's got a squint. And all them pimples.

[*Pause. Church organ lead-in.*]

THREE: Mind you, he always did walk a bit funny, didn't he?

FOUR: He did everything funny.

THREE: Aye. Look. Look at him. You think he'd be ashamed to stand there, wouldn't you? And the other one, on his organ.

FOUR: Mmmm . . . and them choir boys have got rosy cheeks too.

[*They launch into the first verse of* Onward Christian Soldiers.]

[*THE LIGHTS COME UP.*]

Scene One

The TINSLEY *living-room.*

IRENE: Come in, come in, but . . . the shop is open, you know.

THWAITE: Yes, I . . . the fact is . . . ah, is Mr Tinsley about?

IRENE: Yes, come through, come through; sit yourself down. Trevor!

TREVOR: [*off*] WHARRISIT?

[IRENE *goes to the cellar.*]

[*off*] WHARRISIT?

IRENE: It's Mr Thwaite. [*to* THWAITE] He won't be a moment.

[TREVOR *enters from the cellar.*]

TREVOR: Wharris? Oh, Mr Thwaite.

THWAITE: Mr Tinsley, I . . .

IRENE: Will you have a cup?

[*She was making tea.*]

THWAITE: Oh, I . . .

IRENE: Sit down, sit down. I'll just . . .

[*She goes through to the kitchen.*]

THWAITE: It's about your letter, Mr Tinsley.

IRENE: Is it about having our Glenda christened?

THWAITE: No, Mrs . . . ah, it's about a letter your husband sent to me.

[IRENE *leans round the kitchen door.*]

IRENE: Oh yes?

TREVOR: Well, a note, more like, kind of thing.

THWAITE: More than a note, Mr Tinsley. I have received many 'notes' these last few weeks. Anonymous notes. Scribble. But your letter, Mr Tinsley, your letter is the only expression of understanding and support I have received from all this village! And I am deeply, deeply grateful for it.

TREVOR: [*blushing*] Oh . . .

IRENE: Was it about . . . you know?

THWAITE: About the rumours, Mrs Tinsley. About the vile rumours and slanders concerning my behaviour, my alleged behaviour, with Mr Pickering.

IRENE: Oh, yes . . .

[*She goes back into the kitchen.*]

THWAITE: Really, I just, I just felt I had to tell you how *much* your gesture, your letter, meant to me. In this hour of . . . Thank you. Thank you from the very bottom of my heart.

TREVOR: Well . . . I'm not much of a church-goer, but . . . well . . .

THWAITE: There is one small point, though. The . . . tone . . . of your letter rather implied that you did perhaps give some credence to the . . . the claim that Mr Pickering and I were observed in the act of running about on the vicarage lawn, at night. Without clothes on.

TREVOR: What I meant to say . . .

THWAITE: Oh, I understood that your feelings were entirely sympathetic, Mr Tinsley, believe me I did. But I should like to take this opportunity to assure you, to swear to you and promise you that there is absolutely no truth whatsoever in that disgraceful allegation!

[*Pause.*]

TREVOR: Oh . . .

[IRENE *comes in with the tea-tray. She puts it on the table.*]

IRENE: Chocolate biscuits? I know you like them. That's right, sit yourself down.

THWAITE: Ah, thank you, Mrs . . . ah . . .

[IRENE *smiles and goes through into the shop.*]

TREVOR: Well, anyway, the thing is, what I thought was: why not? I mean, I don't see why you shouldn't be as good a vicar as the next man, even if you are that way inclined.

THWAITE: What way inclined?

TREVOR: I mean, I'm not much of a church-goer, but,

it just seems to me you *shouldn't* just run away from here. No, what you should do, you should gerrup, in your pulpit, and stand there, and say: 'Now, it just so happens, I'm an homosexual. That's the way God made me. That's the way I am. So there!' . . . kind of thing.

THWAITE: But, I'm not! I *am not*! Really, I am *not*!

[TREVOR *looks sceptical.*]

TREVOR: Oh, come on!

THWAITE: Oh, God!

[*He cries.*]

TREVOR: Ah, Mr Thwaite, what I'm saying is (and it goes right up to the Bishops!) there's too much hypocrisy about these things. Love . . . and sex. You should stand up for love. I mean, you happen to love another man. Mr Pickering. Well, providing you don't molest little kiddies, why not? Love is love.

THWAITE: No. No . . .

TREVOR: Oh, but it is.

IRENE: [*off*] Trevor! Where's the chocolate biscuits?

TREVOR: They're where they always are!

IRENE: Oh.

TREVOR: Look, what does it say in the Bible? Ah . . . To thine own self be true. So, you're an homosexual. But homosexual love is love, i'n't it? Ah, don't get me wrong now, I'm not that way inclined myself, but . . .

[THWAITE *rushes out through the shop.* TREVOR *sighs and shakes his head.* IRENE *comes back in.*]

IRENE: Trevor, Mr Thwaite's just gone rushing out! Running up the road.

TREVOR: Aye. He's just running away from himself.

IRENE: Oh. Is he all right?

TREVOR: No, Irene, he's not. And how many of us are?

IRENE: Mmm. I've got fig rolls, instead.

[*BLACKOUT. There is the sound of an ambulance klaxon.*]

Scene Two

The TINSLEY *living-room.* TREVOR *and* SGT HARRY ASQUITH *are seated, exchanging occasional sighs and tut-tuts.* IRENE *comes through from the kitchen.*

IRENE: Here we are then. Nice fresh fig rolls. I know you like them.

HARRY: Aye.

[*The tea things are already laid out.* IRENE *pours, hands out cups and sits down.*]

IRENE: Well . . . who'd have thought it?

[*Pause.*]

HARRY: Aye . . . So, he run off back to his vicarage and that's the last you saw of him, is it?

[TREVOR *nods and sighs.*]

IRENE: Yeah. He were waving his arms about a bit. But perhaps that were just his way of running.

HARRY: Hm. Aye. Perhaps.

[TREVOR *sighs.* HARRY *sighs.* IRENE *sighs.*]

Aye.

TREVOR: To thine own self be true, eh?

HARRY: What?

IRENE: He's been saying that ever since.

TREVOR: To thine own self be true.

IRENE: See what I mean?

TREVOR: That's what I said to him, Harry. To thine

own self be true. But he couldn't. Worra way to go, though.

[*He shakes his head.*]

HARRY: Oh. Aye. Er . . . this letter, Trevor. Why did you send it to him?

TREVOR: Well, after all the stories, you know . . .

HARRY: Oh, I know . . .

TREVOR: Well, after all that, and them telling him to keep out of the cricket club changing rooms, and Pickering getting his pants pulled off at that dance . . . well, I thought, he might *need* a bit of encouragement.

HARRY: Oh aye? How do you mean, encouragement?

TREVOR: I mean, uplift, backing, support.

HARRY: Hm. Nice fig rolls, Irene.

IRENE: [*as if she'd made them*] Oh . . .

HARRY: He were a poofter, you know.

TREVOR: Well, that's as maybe . . .

HARRY: Oh, he were. Tried and tested. Pickering's told us all about their little frolics. Bit of a dab hand with a camera, too. 'Art studies' they call them. We had a few red faces down our place, when they went the rounds. Eh? Eh? 'Course I've seen it all before. I was in the army. You know, all the . . . Any road, now, you wrote him the note to encourage him, did you?

TREVOR: I was hoping he'd steel himself to face up to all the hypocrites!

[*Shop bell.*]

IRENE: Oh, I'll go.

[*It's* MRS BALDRY, *a lady in her late 40's or early 50's. She mouths questions: 'Is he in there?' etc. She clutches at* IRENE.]

MRS B: [*whispering*] Is he in there?

IRENE: Shhh.

MRS B: It's in the paper you know.

HARRY: Trevor, a word to the wise. Tread careful, lad. Eh, eh? Friendly letters to suicidal nancy boys, it's not good for trade, is it now? Eh, eh? Be honest.

[*Pause.*]

TREVOR: That man was *hounded* to death! And for why? Eh? For expressing love.

HARRY: Well, in a manner of speaking, quite. Quite. But there's ways and ways, aren't there? And skipping round his lawn in the altogether with young Pickering with flowers behind his ears is not the best way of going about things. That's all I'm saying. Specially not at full moon and when the pubs are chucking out. That's all I'm saying. Don't get me wrong now. I'm not one for saying poofters should have their knackers lopped off. No more than a poor old flasher should. I do *not* go along with that proposal. *But*, well, they could stop at home, couldn't they? And pull the curtains. It's not a matter of what you should do or shouldn't do, or do do or don't do. It's a matter of, if you do it, where you do it, and when you do it. Common sense, that's all.

[*Pause.*]

TREVOR: That man, that *man*, was as good as lynched from his own bell tower!

HARRY: Oh aye, granted, yeah . . . but why? Eh? Ask yourself. Not for being a poofter. If every poofter in the land went and hanged hisself from a bell rope, we'd all be deaf with the clanging. No, no. His trouble were, he were a silly poofter. That's all. A fool. That's all.

[*Pause.*]

TREVOR: And if I speak up for him I'm a fool too, am I?

[*Ching of coins. Sound of cash register. Pause.*]

HARRY: The motto is: mum's the word. If you'd been on the force as long as I have, you'd know. I've seen it all. What? Theft, bash-ups, touch-ups, buggering, rape, little kiddies, old ladies tied to trees . . . murder! Orgies (in the most surprising places). Sheep! The lot! But: mum's the word. I don't go round telling all and sundry. I talk about football, and weather, and holidays. I don't let it affect me *too much.* That's not to say I don't have feelings. I do! And I like a bit of fun as much as the next man. But you can't let it get the better of you, can you? He did. I don't. You mustn't. Mum's the word. Let that be your motto.

[*Pause.*]

TREVOR: And I say to you, Harry Asquith: To thine own self be true.

[*Pause.* MRS BALDRY *leaves the shop.*]

HARRY: Well . . .

[IRENE *comes through from the shop.*]

IRENE: Oooo, they do go on, don't they? Telling me all about how they found him, and how they cut him down, and how his face were all black and the veins standing out. Ugh! Mrs Baldry, she knows no more about it than I do. Were you actually there, Harry? Did you, like, see him? Dangling?

HARRY: I did. Aye. I can tell you this, Irene, he were not a pretty sight. Fair put young Pickering off his dinner, I can tell you. [*he pockets a couple of fig rolls*] Which reminds me, nosh. Eh, eh? Tarra then, I'll see myself out.

IRENE: Tarra, Harry.

HARRY: Tarra, Irene.

[HARRY *leaves through the back door. Pause.* TREVOR *shakes his head. Pause.*]

IRENE: Oh, Trevor, you mustn't brood. I'm sure nobody blames you.

TREVOR: You know . . . what?

IRENE: Nothing. I said don't *brood*.

[TREVOR *shakes his head.*]

TREVOR: You know, Irene, we're still young.

IRENE: . . . Yeah?

TREVOR: But is it going to go on like this? For all the years to come?

IRENE: Well . . .

TREVOR: Glenda growing up, going through school, us going over to self-service, changing cars, longer holidays, weekends, retiring to Scarborough? We're young, Irene. *Young*. But not for very long.

IRENE: Well . . . it's the same for everybody.

[*Shop bell.*]

Oh, I'll go.

[*She goes halfway out, then pops back.*]

Don't go getting *agitated*!

[*She goes into the shop and switches the light on. The customer is* STANLEY BALDRY, *smiling.*]

TREVOR: To thine own self be true.

IRENE: What do you want Stanley?

STANLEY: [*watching the light flicker on*] I don't know!

[*He laughs.* TREVOR *slaps his hands together.*]

TREVOR: To thine *own* self be true!

STANLEY: Not a clue.

[STANLEY *laughs again and leaves.* IRENE *goes into the living-room.*]

TREVOR: Sit down, Irene, I want to talk to you.

IRENE: Oh?

[*She sits down.*]

TREVOR: I was just standing in the kitchen when it came to me, like woosh. And, well, the more you think about it . . . The Quality of Life, I mean . . . round here . . . the more you think about it, the lower it seems. It does. It's very low indeed, really. I mean, mum's the word. I mean, this is the 20th century! It is! This is the result of centuries, hundreds of years, of progress. But it's not much fun, is it? The way we were brought up, for instance. The more I think about the kind of standards we were brought up with, well, the more wrong they seem. All wrong. We're sooo . . . inhibited, aren't we? So shut up in ourselves. Oh, I know . . . that's the industrial revolution for you; that's the heritage of all the puritan thingy . . . I know that, good point, but . . . why do we keep on with it? Really? Why don't we just break loose of all the bad kind of . . . well, ideology, all the stuff we had drilled into us and shoved down our throats at school, and Sunday school, and the cubs and brownies, and at home? I think, if we could break loose, I think we could all be a *lot* happier!

[*Pause.*]

This could be a much happier place, the whole . . . society, if only people were more willing to consider new ideas. To look at themselves, and their lives, and be more adaptable. Flexible. More honest, really. More, well . . . free.

[*Pause.*]

More free in their ways, in their opinions, in their ideas. Less willing to criticize . . . things. Do you know what I mean, Irene?

[*Pause.*]

IRENE: Oh yeah, you mean, in bed.

TREVOR: No! Well, not just . . . no. Everything. Everything.

IRENE: You mean sex, don't you? You mean us. Me.

TREVOR: No! I don't. Well . . . Irene, why do you *always* think I mean . . . sex?

IRENE: Because you do.

[*Shop bell.* TREVOR *is about to answer but goes into the shop. It's* STANLEY.]

TREVOR: How do, Stanley. What can I do for you?

STANLEY: Er, two pennorth of vinegar in a brown paper bag! On tick! Please.

[*Pause.*]

TREVOR: Stanley, who told you to say that?

STANLEY: Jacky said.

TREVOR: Yes, well, you go and tell Jacky Thomas to find something better to do with his time than playing tricks on you.

STANLEY: Haven't you got none?

TREVOR: Stanley, don't let them treat you like this! Stick up for yourself. Say no. Go on now. Say NO!

STANLEY: Yeah. Right. Yeah. NO! Yeah.

[STANLEY *leaves.* TREVOR *goes back into the living-room.*]

TREVOR: I'm talking about life in general! Sex *is* a part

of life, yes, and an important part, too, but . . .

IRENE: Who was it?

TREVOR: Stanley. The thing is, about sex, about love . . .

IRENE: What did he want?

TREVOR: Two pennyworth of vinegar in a brown paper bag, for Jacky Thomas.

IRENE: Oooo, he never learns, does he?

TREVOR: No. Now, about what we were talking about . . .

IRENE: Trevor, I can't change the way I am.

TREVOR: But you could! You can!

IRENE: I can't!

TREVOR: You can. You can!

[IRENE *starts sobbing.*]

IRENE: No. If, if you said: 'Irene, let's leave here, let's pack up shopkeeping' . . . well, I could do that. If you said: 'Irene, let's go and live in a caravan, or on a farm, or emigrate, or why don't you get your hair dyed blue' . . . well, I could. I could do that. But not . . . you know. I can't, Trevor, I can't!

[*Pause.*]

TREVOR: It's about love! It's all about love!

[*Shop bell.*]

Oooooh!

[*He goes into the shop. It's* STANLEY *again.*]

STANLEY: I told him. I told him: NO! He hit me.

TREVOR: Er, well . . .

STANLEY: He kicked me.

[*He puts his leg up on the counter and shows* TREVOR.]

TREVOR: Stanley, never mind. Don't think about it.

STANLEY: It hurts.

TREVOR: Yes, but, I mean . . .

STANLEY: He called me names.

TREVOR: Well, don't listen. Don't listen.

STANLEY: I might be daft, but I'm not deaf.

TREVOR: Yes, but, well, I mean . . . well . . .

[STANLEY *walks out. Pause.* TREVOR *goes back into the living-room.*]

You see, look at it this way . . .

[IRENE *has gone upstairs. Pause.*]

. . . if at first you don't succeed . . .

[*He's almost crying. He throws a plastic toy duck he's been holding at the wall.*]

[*BLACKOUT.*]

[*SOUND ONLY.* TREVOR *and* IRENE *are drinking coffee.*]

TREVOR: Mmm . . . delicious . . . mmm. By gum, Irene, you do make a good cup of coffee.

IRENE: Glenda . . . suck it pet. Don't blow. Suck.

TREVOR: And that bacon. That bacon . . . I defy anyone to do better bacon than you do, Irene. I do! You must have green fingers. I mean it. It's a gift! Lucky me, eh?

[*Pause.*]

Yeah. What? Oh, sorry, I thought you said something.

IRENE: No.

TREVOR: Oh. Well . . .

[*He hums* 'Strangers in the Night'.]

[*LIGHTS UP.*]

Scene Three

The shop. MRS BALDRY *and* STANLEY *are standing waiting.* TREVOR *is in the living-room, holding a paraffin can, reading* 'Ecstasy'. SHIRLEY *enters.* TREVOR *hears the bell and exits out to the back yard.*

MRS B: He won't be long, dear. He's getting me some paraffin.

SHIRLEY: Ah.

[SHIRLEY *smiles and nods. Pause.* STANLEY *stares at her, grinning. She smiles back.* STANLEY *blushes and grins even more.*]

MRS B: I don't know where Irene is. Probably gone to her mother's for a bit of peace and quiet. [*noticing* STANLEY *grinning at* SHIRLEY] Stanley, stop it. Will you stop it. And don't scowl. Yes, you were. It's all right Mrs . . . Smith, i'n't it? [SHIRLEY *nods*] It's all right. He means no harm. He's, you know, a little bit backward. We don't know why. He's a trial, but well, he's all I've got. Mind you, when I've gone, goodness knows what they'll do to him. I shudder to think. His father died prematurely, you see. [*mouthing*] CANCER. Of the bladder. Oh, the things I've seen . . .

SHIRLEY: Yes. Er . . . will he be much longer, do you think?

MRS B: Oh him. He could get lost in his own back yard, him. He comes from a long line of duff-bags. All his lot were a bit funny. His Uncle Godfrey . . . he's named after him. His real name's Godfrey Trevor, only he calls himself Trevor . . . His Uncle Godfrey finished up in a home. He was very peculiar indeed. What they call 'extremely odd'. He had a wooden leg, and he would keep showing it to people. And not just the leg . . . you know . . . and he got worse as he got older. Mind you, they do say it runs in families, don't they? I mean, they seem to think, nowadays, the medical men, that it's in the blood from the moment you're born. And it can lie dormant for years and years. But sooner or later it starts. It multiplies and multiplies, until before very long there's so much of it that it's swimming all through your blood vessels, the veins, all through your body, up and down the arteries, until one fine day it finds its way up into your head, through your neck, and then BINGO it starts eating your brains away.

[STANLEY *makes sucking noises and mimes brains being eaten away.*]

[*giving him a penny*] Here, Stanley, get yourself some bubble gum.

SHIRLEY: [*crossing to the counter*] Well . . .

MRS B: Yes, I mean even as a lad, Trevor Tinsley were a bit peculiar. Odd, you know. You could see it, every now and again. But lately . . . oh, what? And then, his performance last Saturday put the tin lid on it. I've never seen such an exhibition in all my life. In the school hall, they have these discussion groups, they call them the big wigs. The late vicar started them. Him that rung the bells.

SHIRLEY: I don't go to church.

MRS B: Oh, neither do I, dear. Nobody does. And, anyway I was brought up strict Methodist. But any road, last Saturday they were discussing marriage. Yeah. And everybody's standing up saying how sometimes it's good and sometimes it's not so good and some's better than others and there's good and bad in everything, they talk like that, when all of a sudden he gets on his hind legs and he says, this is him: 'Mr Chairman, fellow debators. Er, marriage means monogamy. But, God said: "Love thy neighbour." So, which is it to be?' Well, dead silence. Absolute hush. And then he says: 'I am serious'. Well, that did it; they roared; they laughed and laughed, and he's gesticulating calling them all pig-ignorant, and worse; and the more he yells, the more they laugh. Till finally he stalks out. Leaving Irene to come home on her own. And everybody looking at her. Poor soul. And that's what I mean. Potty. Crackers. Bonkers. Imagine poor Irene though. Imagine living with a loony.

[STANLEY *nods.* SHIRLEY *looks at both of them.* TREVOR *enters the shop with the paraffin and hides behind the counter.*]

Mind you, you have to smile, don't you? Still, it's no laughing matter for Irene. It's her I feel for.

[TREVOR *blows a fart.*]

Stanley!

STANLEY: Hello?

MRS B: Stanley, we are not beasts in the field.

[*As she turns back to speak to* SHIRLEY, TREVOR *blows another fart.*]

Stanley!

STANLEY: Eh?

[*She wags a finger in his face.*]

MRS B: You are supposed to be a little gentleman. Well?

[TREVOR *blows another fart.*]

Right. That's it. Out! Get out!

STANLEY: But . . . but . . .

MRS B: No buts! You get some fresh air inside you. Go on. Out!

STANLEY: It wasn't me, Mum, honest.

[STANLEY *is pushed outside protesting.* MRS BALDRY *smiles at* SHIRLEY.]

MRS B: He's a child at heart.

[SHIRLEY *opens the freezer lid.* TREVOR *blows another fart.*]

SHIRLEY: [*smiling*] Well, it's not me.

MRS B: Well, it's certainly not *me*!

[TREVOR *stands up.*]

TREVOR: Mrs Baldry, your paraffin.

[*She stares at him, mutters, and slams 10p pieces down on the counter.*]

MRS B: You, Mister, you will end up locked up in a prison for silly buggers.

TREVOR: [*smiling*] Have you ever thought, Mrs B, how starved of love we all are? Have you ever thought how little love there is in your life? Behind the lace curtains? Have you ever thought how much love there could be in the world, should be in the world, and how little there is, at the moment? Have you?

MRS B: No, I have not!

TREVOR: Well, I wish you would. In the meanwhile, though, have the paraffin on me, Mrs B. As a small token of my affection.

MRS B: Well, in all my life, I never . . . I pay for what

I want! And I don't want your silly antics! Gobbin! Pillock!

[*She slams the door behind her.* TREVOR *shakes his head and sighs.*]

SHIRLEY: I think you frightened her.

TREVOR: People *are* frightened of ideas, it's quite true. And when it's an idea about love, well . . . But, I'm only saying what I think. I've thought it for a bit, but I've only recently worked up the nerve to *say* what I think. But I honestly *do* think we all need all the love we can get. I honestly think that.

[SHIRLEY *smiles and nods.*]

SHIRLEY: Yeah.

[*Pause.*]

TREVOR: You agree?

SHIRLEY: Mmmm.

TREVOR: You think the same?

SHIRLEY: Yeah. Can I have some margarine?

TREVOR: Right. Yes. You're new up here, aren't you?

SHIRLEY: Yes. We've got one of the new houses, on Alpine Drive. On the corner.

TREVOR: Oh, *yes*. And, you really think I'm right, do you, about how we all need to change ourselves?

SHIRLEY: Mmmm.

TREVOR: More, like, free? Natural? Not, like, repressed, kind of thing?

SHIRLEY: Oh, yes.

TREVOR: More, well, in a manner of speaking, naked like?

SHIRLEY: Definitely.

TREVOR: Well. Well. Well, well . . .

[*Pause. They're smiling.* IRENE *has entered through the back door, and through the kitchen. She leans into the shop.*]

IRENE: I've got the bedsocks! Oh, sorry. I'll put the kettle on.

[*She smiles at* SHIRLEY *and goes through to the kitchen.*]

TREVOR: My wife.

[SHIRLEY *nods.* TREVOR *looks inside the counter cooler.*]

Margarine, margarine . . .

SHIRLEY: Do you do deliveries?

[TREVOR *bangs his head.*]

TREVOR: We do, yes. Yes, I do.

[*They smile.*]

[*BLACKOUT. Sound of The Rolling Stones singing* 'You can't always get what you want'.]

Scene Four

The TINSLEY *living-room. The radio is playing music.* TREVOR *enters from the back yard.* IRENE *enters from the shop having switched off the shop lights and drawn the curtain as she comes in.*

TREVOR: [*switching off the kitchen light*] Are we shut?

[IRENE *nods.*]

Ooof. What a day, eh?

IRENE: It's been terribly quiet.

TREVOR: That's what I mean. Foof!

[IRENE *switches off the radio.*]

IRENE: Trevor: you know, the shop's not been doing very well lately. All things considered . . .

TREVOR: Go on.

IRENE: Well, after, you know, after the Discussion

Group, well . . . people don't *really* like being talked to the way you talk to them.

TREVOR: Go on.

IRENE: Well, if you go in a shop and what you want's a meat pie, or a tube of toothpaste, and somebody asks you what you think about, well, Free Love . . . well, it's bound to make you nervous. I'm only saying.

[*Pause.*]

TREVOR: How about us going for a walk, eh? Up the Reservoir, or Longbottom Wood, and how about us taking all our clothes off, and going running about in the open air? You and me.

IRENE: It's cold. We'd be covered in goose pimples.

TREVOR: And how about us making love like that? In the grass. Just the open sky above us. Eh?

IRENE: Ooo, it'd be all prickly, Trevor. And people might see.

TREVOR: Nobody'd see us on the tops.

IRENE: No, but all them sheep, staring. And bugs. And prickly grass. Thistles. And anyway, it might rain.

[*Pause.*]

TREVOR: Well, then.

[IRENE *goes to the cellar to get the ironing board.* STANLEY *enters from the cellar, holding his hands cupped together.*]

STANLEY: I've got it, Irene. I've got it. Hello, Trev.

[*He exits through the kitchen.*]

TREVOR: Got what?

IRENE: He's been chasing a frog in the cellar.

STANLEY: Tarra.

TREVOR: Oh! Nice.

[STANLEY *comes back, rubbing his hands on his clothes.* IRENE *has set up the board and the iron and starts to do her ironing.*]

STANLEY: Ooo, sticky.

[*He smiles at* TREVOR, *licks his hands and fingers, and sits down. Pause.*]

TREVOR: Are you stopping, Stanley?

STANLEY: Yeah. [*he grins*]

TREVOR: What . . . is . . . going . . . *on*?

IRENE: I'm looking after him while his mother gets back. She's gone to the doctor's about, you know, her rash. The blotches.

TREVOR: Oh. Well . . . I want to talk to you.

IRENE: Well, that's all right. Stanley's all right.

STANLEY: I'm all right.

[*Pause.*]

TREVOR: Right. Right. It's about *Ecstasy*.

IRENE: Oh.

[*He pulls it out from behind the cushion of the chair that* STANLEY'*s sitting on.*]

TREVOR: Have you looked at it?

IRENE: No, love. I haven't. No.

TREVOR: Why not?

[*Pause.*]

Why not?

IRENE: I don't like . . . dirty books.

STANLEY: Oooo.

[*He looks behind the cushion for more.*]

TREVOR: It is *not* dirty! *Nothing* about the human body is dirty!

IRENE: Glenda's nappies are.

TREVOR: I am not talking about Glenda's nappies. I'm talking about . . . sex.

IRENE: I know you are and I wish you wouldn't.

[*Pause.*]

STANLEY: You know, where I go for training, there's a lad sold his head.

TREVOR: Stanley, please, don't . . . You what?

STANLEY: Tommy Todd. Sold his head. For money.

TREVOR: Sold his head who to?

STANLEY: Er . . . hospital. And, when he's dead they'll chop it off.

TREVOR: Yes, well . . .

STANLEY: They want to pickle it, in a big jar. They want to have it on show, for important people to look at. But he doesn't care! He bought us all fish and chips. He gets so much a week, every week, in a brown envelope. He's laughing, i'n't he?

[*Pause.*]

TREVOR: Look, Irene, listen now . . .

STANLEY: They don't want my head. They wouldn't want yours neither.

TREVOR: Good. Glad to hear it. Irene . . .

IRENE: But, why do they want his head, Stanley?

STANLEY: Well, his is a big one. A whopper. It's all, like, swollen. And he's got an hole in the top.

TREVOR: What?

IRENE: You mean, his fontanelle?

STANLEY: An hole. Where it should have closed shut together, the bones . . . it didn't. So he has to wear a plastic lid to stop stuff dropping through into his head.

TREVOR: Stuff?

STANLEY: Rain. Snow. Bird shit.

[*Pause.*]

TREVOR: Irene . . .

STANLEY: His brother, his brother Franky, he tried to sell his head too, but they didn't want to know. Well, he's only a mongol.

[*Pause.*]

There's a girl comes sometimes; she's got no teeth. Never grew none. She can draw blood just with her gums.

[*Pause.*]

Can I leave the room, please?

TREVOR: Good idea. Please do.

[STANLEY *exits, upstairs.*]

IRENE: Ooh. We are lucky, aren't we?

TREVOR: Irene, I'm going to read you something.

IRENE: I won't listen.

TREVOR: 'Dear *Ecstasy*' . . .

IRENE: I'm not listening . . .

TREVOR: 'Dear *Ecstasy*. I am at the end of my tether. My wife is just not interested in improving our mutual technique. I've tried everything, to no avail. We do have intercourse, but it's always the same. Lights out, me on top, her lying with her eyes shut.'

IRENE: And how does he know that if the lights are out?

TREVOR: 'After a few minutes she says: "Have you finished yet?"'

IRENE: Well, I don't say that. I like it.

TREVOR: 'I tried buying some stimulating books, to stimulate her. She burned them. When I showed her your wonderful article about the Multi-Orgasmic Woman, she laughed at me. For her birthday I got her a battery-operated penis. She sent it to a jumble sale.'

IRENE: Well . . .

TREVOR: 'She will not allow cunnilingus, and she said if I ever mention fellatio again, we'll have to get twin beds.'

[*Silence.*]

'I *was* thinking of having an affair with a

young lady across the road, but she moved house before I could ask her. I do *not* want to fall back on women of the streets because I want to preserve my body from disease. But I am now reduced to the following desperate straits (and it can't go on): when my wife is on the late shift (she is involved with local transport), I strip myself naked and rub myself all over with perfumed oil from Persia. (It's not cheap, but it's good stuff.) I then relieve myself by means of a barrel in the back yard. Yes, it has come to that: making love to a bunghole! Please, what can I do? Yours in desperation, Tormented, Ipswich.'

[*Pause.*]

And the psychiatrist who writes the answers says he should see a psychiatrist, otherwise he could become . . . 'hopelessly dependent' . . . on the barrel.

[TREVOR *shuts the magazine and plonks it on the table.* STANLEY *has come quietly downstairs and has been standing behind* TREVOR.]

STANLEY: I have to see a psychiatrist. Well, he has to see me. He doesn't expect much. He don't get much, neither.

TREVOR: You see?

IRENE: See what?

TREVOR: You see what . . . suffering . . . can be caused?

IRENE: Well . . .

TREVOR: Well?

IRENE: Well, I should have thought what he was most likely to suffer from was splinters.

[TREVOR *almost hits her but*

instead he smashes his hand down onto the table scattering the ironing.]

STANLEY: Eh up!

[STANLEY *runs and hides on the cellar steps, shutting the door behind him.*]

TREVOR: You promised me, in church you promised me, and I promised you, to worship each other with our bodies.

IRENE: I do! I do!

TREVOR: You do *not*! You don't, Irene. You don't.

[*Pause.*]

IRENE: Oh, Trevor, it's just . . . the idea of it makes me feel funny. Ugh! I don't mind different . . . positions, but . . . and I know you keep yourself clean, but . . . just think of all them germs and microbes, though. And, a lot of bacteria's invisible you know. Nowadays. Trev?

[*Pause.*]

But, I do love you.

[TREVOR *smashes his hand on the table.*]

Oh, please, love, you'll only hurt your hand. You'll only hurt yourself.

TREVOR: Whose bloody hand is it? Eh? It's my bloody hand! I'll do what I bloody want with my bloody hand!

[*He bangs the table a few more times . . . and has to bite back a yowl of pain.*]

IRENE: Bloody this and bloody that doesn't help.

TREVOR: Well it bloody well helps me! Bugger it, bugger, bugger, bugger and bloody bugger it!

[*He hits the table again.*]

Buggeration! Sodding hell! Sodding hell fire!

Fuck! Fuck! Fuck me rigid with a red hot bargepole! Bollocks! Bollocks with bells on! Fuck, fucking hell, fucking hell fire, fuck a duck, fuck, fuck! Fuck! Fuck! Fuck!

[*Pause.*]

Fuck!

[*He hits the table again . . . and rushes to the cellar door, jerking it open.*]

STANLEY: Has it blown over?

TREVOR: WAAAAAAAA! URGH! AAAAAAAAR!

STANLEY: Oh, heck.

[TREVOR *slams the cellar door shut. Pause. He goes out, slamming the back door.* IRENE *follows.*]

IRENE: You'll catch cold! Trevor, put your scarf on!

[TREVOR *comes back at speed.*]

TREVOR: WHAT? What did you SAY?

IRENE: I said: put your scarf on.

TREVOR: Oh. Oh.

IRENE: Oh, Trevor . . .

[*They hug, crying.* STANLEY *peeps round the cellar door.*]

STANLEY: Aaa. Aaa. That's better. I say rude things, when I get miffed. I say: 'Dogs' Knickers'.

IRENE: Oh, Trevor . . .

TREVOR: Oh, Irene . . .

IRENE: Oh, it is silly, i'n't it? I do love you.

TREVOR: Well, I love you!

IRENE: I know you do.

TREVOR: I do! I do!

IRENE: I know you do! Oh . . .

[*More hugging and crying. Pause.*]

TREVOR: Irene, let's go to bed.

IRENE: What, now!

TREVOR: Now, now! Uh?

IRENE: Er . . . what about Stanley?

STANLEY: I'm all right.

TREVOR: He's all right.

STANLEY: I'm all right.

IRENE: Oh, but . . his mother'll be coming for him. She'll want to talk about her rash. And, my Mum'll be bringing Glenda back.

TREVOR: We can lock the door. Leave them a note.

IRENE: Yes, but . . . they'd know, wouldn't they? They'd know where we were.

TREVOR: We *are* married.

IRENE: Yes, but . . . I don't like people knowing exactly just when we're doing it. You know?

[TREVOR *breaks away.*]

Tonight though, eh?

[*Pause.*]

Well, you have got the deliveries to deliver.

TREVOR: I'm going out.

IRENE: Where?

TREVOR: I'm delivering the deliveries!

[*He goes out, slamming the back door.*]

IRENE: But, your scarf!

[*Pause.*]

Oh. Ooooo . . .

[STANLEY *comes out, looks round, and decides it's safe.*]

STANLEY: Shall I tell you what I'm going to do when my mother's dead and buried? Well, I'm going to paint our house pink. All over. And I'm going to have lady friends coming to visit. And stopping all night, too, sometimes. If they want. A few. But I'll never get wed. They'll only be friends in the night. Because, my mother says I can't get wed because I mustn't have babies. But I can have friends.

[*Pause.*]

IRENE: I'll tell you something, Stanley. If I ever see a barrel in *our* back yard, I shall bung its bunghole up with glue.

[*She gasps at the idea. She giggles.* STANLEY *giggles too.*]

STANLEY: And then say: 'Right, get stuck in.'

[*They laugh.* TREVOR *has been standing in the kitchen doorway. He charges in.*]

TREVOR: I don't think that's very funny!

[*He rushes into the shop, grabs a box of matches and a small cigar.*]

STANLEY: It depends where you're standing!

[STANLEY *laughs even more.*]

IRENE: Oh, Trevor . . .

[TREVOR *comes back from the shop.*]

TREVOR: Where's my scarf? Ah . . . So, you'd like to see me stuck in a barrel, would you?

STANLEY: Yes.

IRENE: No, Trevor . . . I'm not laughing at you, love, I just . . . I love you.

TREVOR: Huh!

IRENE: It's not that I don't feel like . . . going upstairs. I do. I do feel like . . .

TREVOR: Well, d'you know what I feel like? I feel like a whiff. I am in *just* the mood for a whiff.

[*He lights the cigar then burns his hand on the iron accidentally. He exits quickly.*]

IRENE: Oooo, dear. He never has a whiff unless he's in a funny mood. And not funny haha, neither.

STANLEY: Don't worry, Irene. He'll never find a barrel this time of night.

IRENE: No, he won't. No. No, he won't . . .

[*BLACKOUT.*]

Scene Five

The SMITH *living-room. Sinatra's* 'Domani' *draws to a close, with all its false endings, on the stereo.* SHIRLEY *and* TREVOR *sit on chairs either side of a coffee table and a sheepskin rug. They've been drinking Cinzano and admiring the stereo system.* 'Domani' *finally does end and the machine switches itself off.*

SHIRLEY: Another?

TREVOR: Oh, well . . .

[SHIRLEY *signals: Cinzano, not another Sinatra.*]

Oh, well . . .

[SHIRLEY *gives* TREVOR *a drop more Cinzano, and he drinks it.*]

You see, when I say 'commune' I don't mean drugs and long hair and sleeping bags on bare boards. No I don't. You see, when I say 'commune' I mean ordinary people just wanting a bit more than saying 'hello' in the street, or coffee mornings or what have you. Raffles, baby-sitting circles, discussion groups. We are *very* complicated animals. We have needs that . . . well, desires.

[SHIRLEY *sits on the floor near him.*]

Oh, I know people shy away from the word. But we all have them. Desires. I mean, well, you know . . . commune, sharing . . .

SHIRLEY: I don't think I'd like to share my new kitchen.

More ice?

TREVOR: Oh, well . . .

[SHIRLEY *collects the ice bucket and* TREVOR *plays with a table lamp which appears to come to pieces in his hands and just as quickly re-assembles itself.*]

Ah.

SHIRLEY: Excuse fingers.

TREVOR: Of course.

SHIRLEY: More Cinzano?

TREVOR: Oh, well . . . thank you . . . Shirley.

[*They drink.*]

Or then again, take 'free love'. You mention 'free love', and people run away.

[SHIRLEY *doesn't.*]

And yet, what does it mean? It means, open-hearted. It means affection. It means honesty. *And* . . . sex, yes, but, 'free' doesn't mean irresponsible. No. It doesn't mean jumping on women in the street. No, it doesn't. It means . . . well . . . it all comes back to monogamy. It does. Jealousy, guilt: monogamy. It's a terrible word.

[SHIRLEY *smiles.*]

Anyway, how are you settling in up here?

SHIRLEY: Oh, very well. A bit cut off from friends we used to have but you can soon make new friends, can't you?

TREVOR: Oh, you can, you can. You can. Yes. But, er, does your husband work nights?

SHIRLEY: [*smiling*] He works late, but not all night.

TREVOR: Shirley, I didn't say that meaning . . . you know.

[SHIRLEY *smiles.*]

Well, I did, but . . . Shirley, what do you think of me?

SHIRLEY: I don't think you're happy.

TREVOR: You *can* tell, can't you? Well, you're right. I'm not.

[*Pause. He's not going to make a move, so . . .*]

SHIRLEY: Trevor, I'm not monogamous.

TREVOR: Oh. Oh.

[*She smiles, kisses him lightly, starts undressing and kneels on the rug.* TREVOR *jumps up nervously.*]

Oh. Er . . . oh. I mean, it's not that I . . . I mean . . . I mean yes. I mean YES!

[SHIRLEY *dims the lights and lies on the rug.* TREVOR *starts ripping his clothes off and is finally revealed in Y-fronts only. He tugs at his wedding ring.* SHIRLEY *laughs.*]

[*BLACKOUT. Sound of Sinatra singing* 'Strangers in the Night'.]

Scene Six

The SMITH *living-room. Later.* 'Strangers in the Night' *fades out.* SHIRLEY *and* TREVOR *are wearing matching dressing-gowns . . . he's in* ERIC'*s three-quarter length. Prostrate, dozing.* SHIRLEY *pours Cinzano into* TREVOR'*s glass, balanced on his chest, and clinks his glass with hers.*

SHIRLEY: [*yawning*] To sex.

TREVOR: Oh, yeah. Yeah.

[*He gulps his drink.*]

Oh, wasn't it wonderful though! Eh? Wasn't it just wonderful? Er, it was, wasn't it?

[SHIRLEY *smiles, nods, and yawns.*]

And it was so natural, wasn't it? *Spontaneous*! Oh, wonderful! In all my life, I've never felt so uninhibited. It's just that, that Irene wouldn't understand. How very natural it was. She'd never, *never* understand.

[*He pours himself another drink.*]

'Tormented in Ipswich' was quite right to complain.

[*He drinks.*]

It wasn't wrong at all. It was right. It was *just* the right thing to do. I don't feel guilty though.

SHIRLEY: [*laughing*] Oh, Trevor . . .

TREVOR: What?

[SHIRLEY *laughs and shakes her head.*]

Er, would you go away with me?

SHIRLEY: For a weekend?

TREVOR: No – forever.

[*Pause.*]

I'm only asking.

SHIRLEY: But . . . what for?

TREVOR: Er, well, to live together. And . . .

SHIRLEY: Oh, I couldn't live without Eric. I couldn't leave Eric. And you couldn't leave Irene, could you?

TREVOR: Well, it'd be a bit of a struggle . . .

SHIRLEY: Anyway, we've got a joint mortgage. And you've got the shop.

TREVOR: Urrr, that bloody shop. My savings are in there. Not that *I* care, but . . .

SHIRLEY: And anyway, me and Eric, Eric and me, well . . . you know.

TREVOR: Oh, yeah, anyway, I do *not* feel I've done anything I should not have done. I do *not* feel guilty.

[*Pause.*]

Oh, doesn't it feel wonderful though, when you're completely naked, not even a wedding ring, all coiled up with another body? Oh, i'n't it a wonderful thing, really, making love? I'n't it smashing? Smashing. It's perfect. Perfect. I'm full of the joys of fucking!

[*A door opens and shuts, off.*]

What's that?

ERIC: [*off*] It's only me!

TREVOR: Oh.

SHIRLEY: It's only Eric.

TREVOR: Oh, bloody Emma!

[*He leaps up and scrabbles his clothes together.*]

SHIRLEY: Trevor, don't run away.

TREVOR: No, no, I'm not, I'm not. I just . . . I have to be getting home now, Shirley. Thank you, thank you . . .

[*He dives out of the window.*]

And, thank you! Thank you!

[*He's running away outside.*]

SHIRLEY: Mind the rose bushes!

TREVOR: [*off*] AAAARGH!

SHIRLEY: Oh dear.

TREVOR: [*off, running back to the window with the dressing-gown*] I'm all right, goodbye, goodbye . . . au revoir . . .

SHIRLEY: Oh, like 'The Last of the Mohicans.'

[ERIC *comes in from the kitchen.*]

ERIC: Hey. What, no cocoa?

SHIRLEY: Hello, love, I'm sorry. I'll get it for you.

[*She kisses him on her way through to the kitchen.* ERIC *sits down, relaxes, then finds he's sitting on* TREVOR*'s socks. He holds them up and sniffs them.*]

ERIC: Oh well, clean feet.

[*There is a knock on the front door.* ERIC *opens it, taking the socks with him.*]

Forgot your socks, did you? Oh.

MRS B: Mr Smith, Mr Smith, thank God you're back. Thank *God*! I must tell you. I *must* tell you.

[*She shoves her way inside.*]

ERIC: Aye, come in.

MRS B: I was on my way home from the surgery, and I was walking past, admiring your garden – he's wrecked your roses – and I was walking by, minding my own business, when . . . I saw them, Mr Smith. At it! Curtains wide open . . . at it! In their birthday suits! Together! Doing . . . doing things!

[*Pause.*]

ERIC: Oh aye?

MRS B: In full view! Full view! And, I waited, Mr Smith, I waited under your tree, and I . . . I wanted just to run home and be sick I did, but I forced myself to stay, to tell you, Mr Smith. Trevor Tinsley! In the pink! Running across your garden! I saw it all, Mr Smith. I saw it all! And it was disgraceful! I had to tell you, I had to tell you. Nothing on! And OH! the things they were doing. Your wife! Your wife!

[*Pause.*]

ERIC: Aye. Well, if it gives her pleasure, there's no harm done, is there?

[*Pause.*]

MRS B: WHAT?

ERIC: [*smiling*] Goodnight, Mrs . . .

[SHIRLEY *leans through from the kitchen.*]

SHIRLEY: Baldry.

ERIC: Goodnight, Mrs Baldry.

SHIRLEY: [*smiling*] 'Night, Mrs Baldry.

[MRS BALDRY *gapes, tries to speak . . . squeaks, squawks, manages one great grunt . . . and flees. She slams the door.* ERIC *and* SHIRLEY *smile at each other.*]

ERIC: Well, takes all sorts to make a world, doesn't it?

SHIRLEY: I do *love* you.

ERIC: Oh, good.

[*They laugh and kiss.*]

[*BLACKOUT.*]

Scene Seven

A tight spot on TREVOR, *naked, with a bundle of clothes. He drops them then starts putting them on. He's looking round all the time.*

TREVOR: [*singing*] 'Softly – I will leave you to softly . . .' I don't care. It was right. It was right, it was right, it was just the right thing to do. Casanova. I was immaculate. Follow that, Eric. Float like a butterfly, sting like a bee. Ow!

[*He's trapped his cock in his fly zip.*]

Underpants, you fool. Underpants.

[*He takes his trousers off again, puts his underpants on, then his trousers on again.*]

Hee hee. The nightlife of a grocer, eh? Hee hee. Socks, socks . . .

[*He grubs about but can't find them.*]

Oh no, Oh no . . . I must have dropped them somewhere. I know what I'll do, I'll nip upstairs, quick. Put on another pair – and no one will be any the wiser. Wedding ring! Wedding ring!

[*He finds the ring in a pocket, and puts it on.*]

Like a bloody noose around my neck. Huh. I've a good mind to throw it away.

[*He doesn't. He sniffs instead. He takes a deep breath and then saunters off, singing* 'Strangers in the Night'. *He laughs loudly on exit.*]

[*BLACKOUT.*]

Scene Eight

The TINSLEY *living-room.* IRENE *and* MRS BALDRY *are sitting at the table. Long silence.*

MRS B: 'Well, if it gives her pleasure'. Huh! I ask you! I ask you!

[*Silence.*]

'No harm done, eh?' Tscha! Tuff! And his little piggy eyes, smirking.

[*Silence.*]

I felt it was my *duty* to tell you, Irene.

[*Silence.*]

IRENE: You must say nothing more about it. I want you to promise me.

MRS B: But what are you going to do?

IRENE: Will you promise me? To say nothing to nobody?

[*Pause.*]

Will you promise me?

MRS B: Oh, you can count on me, Irene, but . . .

IRENE: Thank you.

MRS B: But, pet, what are you going to do?

[*Pause.*]

What *are* you going to do?

[*Silence.* MRS BALDRY *gives up, and, shaking her head, goes to the cellar, and knocks on the door.*]

Stanley?

STANLEY: Can I come out now?

[STANLEY *peeps round the cellar door with* 'Ecstasy' *magazine.*]

MRS B: Come on. We're going home. What's that?

STANLEY: *Ecstasy.*

MRS B: I beg your pardon! Have you been trying to read this?

STANLEY: No.

MRS B: Good.

STANLEY: Just looking at the pictures.

MRS B: Huh? Oh! Oh my sainted aunt!

[*She snaps the magazine shut.*]

STANLEY: I'd like to see a lady breast-feeding a baby.

MRS B: One more word out of you and I'll wash your mouth with soap and water! Home! Home!

STANLEY: Mother, what's . . . what's cunnilinger and fladdio?

MRS B: What are you talking about?

[TREVOR *has entered behind her, through the back door.*]

TREVOR: Just sucking and licking, Stanley. Just sucking and licking. Evening all.

[*He goes upstairs singing* 'Beautiful Dreamer'.]

STANLEY: [*puzzled, then . . .*] Oh! Well, I never did.

MRS B: I should bloody well think not! Out! Go on! Home! Go on!

[*She pushes him through the kitchen, out of the back door.*]

I, I just . . . oh, goodnight, Irene. Goodnight! I shall pray for you.

[IRENE *stares at her.* MRS BALDRY *grunts, and leaves, slamming the door. Pause.* TREVOR *comes back from upstairs.*]

TREVOR: Er, I can't find my slippers.

IRENE: They're there.

TREVOR: Oh. Oh, yeah.

IRENE: Where they always are.

TREVOR: Oh, silly me.

[*He puts his slippers on. He's got new, odd, socks on, but doesn't notice. Pause.*]

All right?

IRENE: Yeah.

TREVOR: Uh-hm.

[*Pause.*]

How's her rash? Mrs B? Coming along? Going away?

IRENE: Same. I don't know. Same.

TREVOR: Ah.

[TREVOR *tries whistling* 'Rose

Marie', *cracks his knuckles and pulls some knitting out of the side of the chair. He goes 'Aaaa' and pulls the needles out, stuffs the knitting away again, crosses his legs, notices his socks don't match, and tucks one foot under himself. He smiles at* IRENE.]

IRENE: I'm tired. Goodnight.

TREVOR: Yes, I'll just, have a bath and . . . I'm sorry I took so long delivering, love. Had a bit of a bump. Nothing serious.

IRENE: Goodnight.

TREVOR: G'night, love. Pet.

[*She's gone upstairs.* TREVOR *regards his socks.*]

No trouble, eh? We got away with it, lads. The question is: what am I going to do? The question is: do I tell Irene? And if I do: when? And how? And another question is: where did I drop my socks? And how much does Eric notice? And how big is he? And is he violent? I don't think he's all *that* big, judging from his dressing-gown. But, little men can be very violent. They're famous for it, some of them. Oh hell. Hell fire.

[*He picks up* 'Ecstasy'. *Stares at it. Rips it up. Suddenly stops.*]

But it was *good*! It was wonderful! At the time. Oooo . . . What I'll do, I'll keep calm. Detached. I'll wait and see. I'll play it cool. And, I'll have another whiff.

[TREVOR *runs towards the shop.*]

[*BLACKOUT.*]

[*SOUND ONLY. Baby* GLENDA *is grizzling.*]

IRENE: Oooh dear, who's a tired baby?

[*Baby gurgles.*]

Yes you are, aren't you? And did your Daddy wake you up, did he? Mmm, I know. He's a silly daddy, i'n't he? He is. He's a flaming nuisance. Never mind. Come on, pet, you just settle down again. Never mind your silly Daddy. You just ignore him. Right?

[*Baby burps.*]

That's right. You tell him what you think of him.

[*LIGHTS UP.*]

Scene Nine

The TINSLEY *living-room.* IRENE *is humming and cooing to* GLENDA, *getting her to sleep in the pram in the back yard.* TREVOR *is in the kitchen.*

IRENE: Yes, you're a little bobby-dazzler aren't you? Well you just settle down.

[IRENE *turns to come inside.* TREVOR *quickly enters the living-room and sits down.* IRENE *enters.*]

TREVOR: Nice day. Outside.

[*Pause.* TREVOR *sighs. Shop bell rings.*]

A customer! A customer!

[*He goes through into the shop. It's* SHIRLEY.]

Oh.

SHIRLEY: Hello.

TREVOR: Hello.

SHIRLEY: I've brought your socks back.

[TREVOR *grabs the socks and fluffs about wondering where to hide them. He stuffs them into the till.*]

TREVOR: Oh. Yeah. Thanks. Shirley. Er, is everything . . .?

[*He nods his head. She shakes hers.*]

Oh, hell. Is, is he after me?

SHIRLEY: Who? Eric? Oh no, Eric's not like that.

TREVOR: Not like what?

SHIRLEY: Eric's not jealous.

TREVOR: He's not?

SHIRLEY: No . . . He's lovely.

TREVOR: Oh. Oh, well you live and learn. Oh.

SHIRLEY: But, Mrs Baldry saw us. Saw you. Streaking.

[*Pause.*]

TREVOR: Eh? Eh?

[IRENE *comes into the shop, behind* TREVOR.]

SHIRLEY: I'll have a packet of digestives, please.

TREVOR: What?

SHIRLEY: A packet of digestive biscuits.

TREVOR: A packet of . . .? Oh! Oh, yes. Yes.

[*He smiles at* IRENE *and edges past her, looking for biscuits.* SHIRLEY *smiles at* IRENE, *who tries to smile back.*]

SHIRLEY: Good morning.

TREVOR: Er, good morning! Oh . . .

[*He produces the biscuits.*]

SHIRLEY: And a half pound of cheddar, please.

TREVOR: Right. Right . . .

[*He gets the cheese out, then fumbles round looking for the knife.*]

SHIRLEY: Looks set for a smashing weekend, doesn't it?

TREVOR: Yes. Oh yes . . .

[IRENE *grabs the knife and* TREVOR *leaps away. She cuts the cheese neatly and fiercely, leaves the knife quivering in the cheese, and walks out.*]

Oh, bloody hell, bloody hell . . .

SHIRLEY: Does she know?

TREVOR: Mrs bloody Baldry was here last night. Before I got back.

SHIRLEY: Oh, well, she knows then.

TREVOR: Oh, bloody hell and buggeration . . .

SHIRLEY: Trevor, I'd best leave you alone.

TREVOR: No! Please, don't . . . er . . .

SHIRLEY: It's for the best, Trev. Let me know what happens. Oh, and if you like, I mean if it's possible, why don't you suggest you both come round for a drink tonight?

TREVOR: A drink? Eh?

[STANLEY *comes in.*]

SHIRLEY: Hello.

STANLEY: Hello.

SHIRLEY: Tarra.

STANLEY: Tarra.

[SHIRLEY *leaves.*]

TREVOR: Shirley, I don't . . . understand . . .

[TREVOR *goes to the door and* STANLEY *traps him behind it, pinning him against the wall.*]

STANLEY: Hello, Trev.

TREVOR: What?

STANLEY: Sucking and licking, eh? Sucking and licking . . .

TREVOR: Er, what, what do you want, Stanley?

[TREVOR *escapes from behind the door.*]

STANLEY: [*shutting the door*] Nothing. I just come to tell

you my mother says I'm never to set foot in here never no more. Not for no reason at all.

TREVOR: Oh. Eh?

STANLEY: Her rash is getting worse. It's all purple, and itchy. In the night it reached right up round her neck, and right down round her knees. She's shitting bricks, I can tell you. She says it's you caused it. She's coated in ointment. Do you reckon she might die of it, Trev? Can you die of a rash?

TREVOR: What? No. No, no . . .

STANLEY: Oh. Well . . . I can't stop talking to you. I'm going to get a white mouse. For company. Tarra.

[*He leaves.*]

TREVOR: Yeah, yeah . . . I don't . . . I don't know what to do! Oh, sodding rotten hell. Oh . . .

[*Offstage a van door bangs; there's singing, then* DESMOND, *the bread man, comes in.*]

DESMOND: 'Lipstick on your collar,
Told a tale on you-hoo,
Lipstick on your collar,
Told you were untrue-hoo.'
Good morning, good morning, Good mor-hor-ning!

TREVOR: Oh no . . .

DESMOND: Eh! Feller on a beach, doing press-ups, keep fit merchant, up and down, up and down, up and . . . and this old feller's walking past, and he stops, and he looks, and he looks . . . up and down, up and down . . . and he starts laughing. And the press-up feller, he says, up and down, up and down: 'What are you laughing at?' Up and down . . . and the old feller says: 'Eeeee, you fool, can't you see she's got fed up of waiting? She's gorrup and gone home!' Eh? Eh? Harra! Harra! Hey-hey! Eh? Ooooo! Cracker, eh?

[*Pause.*]

Right then, Skipper, what'll it be? Brown, white, sliced, muffins, tea-cakes, fancy fingers, twists, cobs, Danish, granary. Eh? I say! Eh?

[IRENE *comes in.*]

IRENE: We don't want anything today, thank you, Desmond.

DESMOND: Oh, hello love. What, nothing?

IRENE: No, thank you, Desmond. Trade is a little bit slack at the moment.

DESMOND: Oh. Right. Cakes?

IRENE: Nothing, thank you, Desmond.

DESMOND: Oh. Well, right. Well, see you Monday then.

IRENE: I don't think we shall require anything Monday either, thank you, Desmond.

DESMOND: Oh. Is everything all right?

IRENE: No.

DESMOND: Oh! Well, not to worry. I'll pop in Monday any road. I'll be going by, you never know, bring you a smile and a song, can't I? Eh?

IRENE: You're a cheerful person, Desmond.

DESMOND: Yes, well . . . yeah.

IRENE: Goodbye.

DESMOND: Yeah. Right. Au revoir! Yeah.

TREVOR: Two dozen cream puffs!

DESMOND: What?

TREVOR: Two dozen cream puffs. Have you got them?

DESMOND: I've got everything, but . . . your good lady said . . .

TREVOR: Two dozen cream puffs! Please.

DESMOND: Right. Pronto. Right.

[*He goes out. Silence. He comes back with the cream puffs.*]

In the back?

TREVOR: No. There.

[DESMOND *puts the cakes on the counter.*]

Thank you.

DESMOND: Pleasure.

[TREVOR *takes the cakes out of the tray, lines them up along the counter, on top of the cash register . . . carefully, neatly.*]

Eh? What you doing? Eh? What's he doing? You can tell me. What are you doing?

IRENE: He's only trying to impress you, Desmond.

[*She walks out as* TREVOR *thumps the first puff. He walks along the counter, thumping each one with a clenched fist, splattering them, like a machine franking stamps, slowly at first, then faster.* DESMOND *laughs at first, but soon stops.*]

DESMOND: Eh? Eh! Don't! Stop it! Stop . . . it.

TREVOR: Ah. I feel better now.

DESMOND: Them's my cream puffs! Them!

TREVOR: How much do I owe you?

[*He produces the socks from the cash register. He stuffs them back in and gets money out.*]

DESMOND: Look, you, look . . . cream puffs are not made for you to flatten them! They're made for eating!

TREVOR: There you are. Keep the change.

DESMOND: People make them! People work hard to make them perfect!

TREVOR: Look, they were my cream puffs, bought and paid for. I'll do what I like with my cream puffs.

DESMOND: They're individually made! To a recipe! We've won medallions for them! They're not made for fun! People work their fingers to the bone making them! People get up at all hours of the night, before dawn, fifty weeks a year, just to make them properly and carefully and well! Our staff take pride in their work! We've got a reputation you know! We don't make rubbish! We make quality confectionery! And we do *not* make it for bloody crackpots to shove their fists through! There's people starving you know, on the streets of Bombay there's people starving, would give their right arms for what you've just flattened!

[*He scoops up some of the cream.*]

They're made with real eggs, you know. Real eggs! Not powdered! Eh? Eh? Eh?

TREVOR: [*sighing*] I'll have another two dozen, please. And six eclairs.

[*Slight pause.*]

DESMOND: You *bloody*, jumped-up, pig-ignorant, squinty-eyed, git's son of a cack-handed, two-faced, *flea-bitten* . . .

TREVOR: Get off my counter!

[*He bangs the counter flap down on* DESMOND*'s fingers.*]

Get back! I'll . . . I'll squirt you! I will!

[*He's grabbed a washing-up liquid bottle.*]

DESMOND: When I've finished with you, you'll look like a cream puff!

TREVOR: Will you . . . Right! I gave you fair warning, Desmond.

[*He squirts.* DESMOND *bellows, falls back . . . it stings his eyes.*]

DESMOND: You bloody savage!

[TREVOR *hands him his tray back, opens the door, and then strides back behind his counter.*]

TREVOR: They were my cream puffs. Bought and paid for, and I have a perfect right to do what I want with my cream puffs.

DESMOND: Nobody has the right to flatten cream puffs! Nobody!

[*He advances on* TREVOR, *who threatens him with the washing-up liquid again.*]

TREVOR: Get back. Get back!

[DESMOND *puts the tray up as a shield.*]

DESMOND: Ah! Haha . . .

TREVOR: Eh!

DESMOND: What?

[DESMOND *lowers the tray, and* TREVOR *squirts him. In agony,* DESMOND *drops the tray, on his foot. He hops about, rubbing his eyes.*]

Right. Right then.

[*He chases behind the counter and starts knocking goods off the shelves.*]

TREVOR: Oh, go on, go on, destroy everything. Go on, I don't care. You think I care? I don't care.

DESMOND: Nobody insults Ainsley's confectionery and gets away with it!

TREVOR: What about them apples, eh? Who do you think spent two hours sticking them up, eh? Cleaning and polishing them, eh? Me. Me!

[DESMOND *grins, then knocks the pyramid of apples flying.* TREVOR *roars, rushes at* DESMOND *and catches him by his coat-tails as he tries to run out. They run on the spot.* DESMOND *escapes.*]

Ha! And good riddance too. Coward! Burke! Twit!

[*He suddenly freezes, backs away from the door, then empties bubble-gums onto the floor.* DESMOND *enters with his arms, pockets, hands and mouth full of muffins and cob loaves.* DESMOND *skids on the bubble-gums and falls. He chucks the bread at* TREVOR *who ducks behind the counter, dodges, etc. . . . Finally* DESMOND *leans on the counter, out of ammo.*]

I don't know what you're trying to achieve, Desmond, *but* . . .

[DESMOND *slaps him in the face with a handful of cream from the counter. Pause.*]

Right. Right! You've asked for it now.

[TREVOR *races over to the frozen food compartment and reaches inside. He finds a giant pack of frozen peas.*]

DESMOND: I've got a van full of stuff out there, you know!

TREVOR: Yes and I've got a shop full of stuff here too!

[*He peppers* DESMOND *with frozen peas. A dreadful weapon.*]

DESMOND: Right! Right! The custards!

[*He rushes out.* TREVOR *grabs a big salami sausage and crouches behind the open shop door, ready to whack* DESMOND. IRENE *enters, behind him.*]

IRENE: Trevor?

[TREVOR *leaps up, poised to clobber her.*]

Put that poloni down.

TREVOR: He . . . he started it.

IRENE: Put that poloni back where it belongs!

[*He does, sulkily.* IRENE *shuts the shop door, just in time to knock a big custard into* DESMOND*'s face. She bolts the door.*]

DESMOND: Eh! Eh! Open up! Coward! Cowardy custard! Chicken! Cock-a-doodle-doo!

IRENE: Desmond, go away.

DESMOND: Nobody . . .

[IRENE *drops the door window-blind.* DESMOND *charges round to the main window.*]

Nobody insults my confectionery and gets away with it!

IRENE: Desmond, go away. Go . . . away.

DESMOND: There'll be no more bread crosses your door-step, Tinsley. Not one loaf. Not a . . .

[IRENE *drops the shop window-blind.* DESMOND *charges to another window.*]

Not a slice. Not a crumb! Ha! So there! Huh? So there!

IRENE: Desmond, I am very sorry if you've been upset, but please go away.

[*She draws the window-blind.* DESMOND *then goes to the shop door.*]

DESMOND: Upset? Upset? Bloody vandal! He gave me

money. Does he think money's everything, does he? Does he think a master-baker has no pride? Eh? Well, he has.

[DESMOND *shoves ripped-up pound notes through the letter box. He's almost crying.* IRENE *goes into the living-room, switching the shop lights off.*]

Does he realise that quality confectionery is my life's work? Eh? No. Well, bloody cowardy custard. Bloody toad in the hole. Bloody mangle-wurzle. Bloody . . . bloody puffed-up pomegranate! Ha! Eh? Huh. So . . .

[DESMOND*'s finger comes through the letter box, pointing accusingly.*]

Let that be a lesson to you, Tinsley. Do NOT meddle with bakers! Let that be a warning to you. [*he gets his arm stuck*] Give me my bloody arm back. Huh. Yeah. What? Yeah. Hur! Yeah, right, hur. So. There. Eh? Yeah. Eh? Yeah. [*he frees his arm*] You bloody orangutang. Yeah, bloody, bloody . . . crumpet-buttock! . . . bloody, bloody, bloody . . .

[*Pause. Silence.* DESMOND*'s van is heard, starting up, being crunched into gear, and screaming away. Pause.* TREVOR *shuts the frozen food compartment, chucks his shop-coat onto the floor, puts the counter lights off, sees eggs and says 'Aahh' in disappointment at not having used them and goes through into the living-room, still with cream on his face. Pause.*]

TREVOR: I'm sorry.

[*Pause.*]

I'm sorry, Irene.

[*Pause.*]

IRENE: Sorry what for?

TREVOR: For . . . fighting. And . . . oh. Oh . . .

[*A long silence.*]

Why didn't you say something last night?

IRENE: She seems . . . very nice. Attractive.

TREVOR: She's married! She loves her husband! I love you!

[*Pause.*]

They've invited us round for a drink!

[TREVOR *realises that wasn't perhaps the right moment . . .*]

Irene, *please*! Please, don't just sit there!

[*Pause.*]

Say something. Say it! *Say* it . . .

[*Pause, or silence.*]

IRENE: I've not got nothing to say. Can say. I don't know what to say. Except . . . it'll be a bit . . . complicated . . . with the shop. With the shop being in both our names. And . . . Glenda, and . . . I know I'm not much, you see. My mum'd be on the rampage now, but . . . it's not the . . . end of the world, and . . . I'm not like my mum. I'm . . . I'm very ordinary, I know . . . I'm not very bright, clever . . . and I'm not *really* interested in improving myself and . . . really, and . . . not much to look at, either, and . . . I have been very wrapped up in the baby but . . . I *never* wanted anything very much, I *never* wanted much, I always just wanted what . . . just what other people . . . wanted. Ordinary things. To be like everybody else. Just ordinary. P'raps, even, boring, really . . . I can see how anybody would find me, dull . . . and boring, and . . . I daresay

I am. I am! And, I'm certainly not much of a sex-pot. But . . . even cooking, I'm only . . . I'm ordinary. Nothing special. Even make-up, choosing clothes, I never know . . . what to do. Got, not got, not, much sense of . . . not stimulating, not daring. Just, ordinary again. Not . . . never once exciting. Never once. Plain. Ordinary. And dull. Yeah. That's all. Me. That's all I've got to say. I've not got nothing to say about . . . about anything. That's me. That's all.

[*Pause.*]

TREVOR: Irene, that's terrible!

IRENE: Oh, yeah, I'm sorry. I can . . . I can understand how . . . how you can, must, find me . . . not enough. Because . . . I'm probably not. Probably not enough.

TREVOR: Irene, shut up.

IRENE: Probably not. No. I'm sorry, but I am. Dull.

TREVOR: Oh, shut up, shut up. I love you. *Shut up*!

IRENE: I am sorry about it, me, but . . .

TREVOR: SHUT UP! Shut up! Irene . . . I love you. I do. I do.

IRENE: [*smiling*] Thank you for saying it . . . Sorry though. Sorry.

TREVOR: IRENE, DON'T BE SO BLOODY HUMBLE!

IRENE: You're, yes, you're quite right to shout. I'm sorry though. I'm sorry . . .

TREVOR: OOOOOOH!

[IRENE *is shaking, trying not to cry or scream.* TREVOR *screams, grabs a rucksack from the top of the cellar, rushes into the shop, and grabs tins, bottles and bread off the floor. He chucks them into the ruck-*

sack, grabs his coat, rushes into the living-room and out to the kitchen . . . then back. He grabs some more things from the shop and rushes back into the living-room.]

Don't think I'm running away! I am not running away!

[*He runs away. Pause.*]

IRENE: Oh . . .

[*Pause. She picks up a toy from the floor.*]

Still, even so . . . still. It's not the end of the world, is it?

[*She breaks down, cries, and howls.*]

[*FAST BLACKOUT.*]

Scene Ten

The TINSLEY *living-room. Dark. There is a tapping on the door. Pause. The door opens and is quietly closed.* STANLEY *switches his torch on, shining it on himself.*

STANLEY: It's only me. Stanley. Shall I put the light on?

TREVOR: No.

[STANLEY *finds* TREVOR *with his torch . . . he's huddled up, squatting on the floor.*]

Hello, Stanley. I'm back.

STANLEY: Yeah. I didn't think you'd emigrate. I saw you just now, crossing the road.

TREVOR: Is Irene at her mother's?

STANLEY: Yeah. Ooo, she cried and cried. And shivered too. Still, she'll be wrapped up in a warm bed now though.

TREVOR: I've been crying too. Walking. Thinking.

STANLEY: I didn't get my white mouse neither. They'd sold out! Still, I can try again next week.

[*Pause.*]

Still not sorted nothing out then?

TREVOR: No.

STANLEY: Oh.

TREVOR: I'm back where I started from.

[*Pause.* STANLEY *sits next to* TREVOR *on the floor, sharing* TREVOR*'s cigarette.*]

STANLEY: Do you know, I've never had a fuck. Never, not once. I know what to do; more or less. But I've never done it. There's a girl where I go, for training, and she's never done it neither. She has something with a long name. Fits. We talk about it. I say: 'Ee Annabelle, I would like to fuck you'. And she says: '*Well*, I'd like to fuck you too'. But we never get the chance. There's a feller goes round saying: 'Hey stop that'. He earns his living stopping fucking. [*pause*] Full time. Eeh dear. A good cry's all right for a bit, but it doesn't last long, does it?

TREVOR: No.

STANLEY: You can't go *on* crying, can you?

TREVOR: No.

[*Pause.*]

MRS B: [*off*] Hello? Hello?

STANLEY: My mother! I'm not to talk to you.

[*He goes to the cellar.*]

Oh, sod this cellar! I'll go in the shop.

[*He goes, leaving the cellar door open.* MRS BALDRY *enters, with a torch. She finds* TREVOR.]

Dogs' knickers.

MRS B: Hello, you're back.

TREVOR: [*sighing*] Yeah, I'm back.

[*Pause.*]

MRS B: Yes, my rash is no better.

[*Pause.*]

Can I talk to you?

TREVOR: [*sighing*] Yes. What about?

[*Pause.*]

MRS B: About me. About love. You talk about love. I'm talking about love too.

[*Pause.*]

TREVOR: Er, well, the thing is . . .

MRS B: About bodies. Trevor? When do you think I first saw my husband's body? When I nursed him. When he was dying. When his body was sick. Shrinking. That's the only man I ever saw, naked. Dying. Trevor, I'm asking you. Please? Please love me. Please love *me*?

[TREVOR*'s got up and is backing round the room, being stalked, ending up at the cellar door.*]

TREVOR: What? Er, no, you see, the thing is, really . . .

MRS B: Trevor, please!

TREVOR: No, please . . . please, no . . .

MRS B: Please, yes!

TREVOR: Please, no! Please . . . no!

MRS B: Oh, Trevor . . .

[TREVOR *yells . . . and falls down the cellar steps. There are bumps, a thud, and a moan.*]

Trevor! Where've you gone? What've you done? Trevor!

[STANLEY *has entered from the shop. He switches the cellar lights on.*]

STANLEY: He's fell down the cellar.

MRS B: Stanley!

STANLEY: He's trod on a frog, most likely.

MRS B: Oh, Stanley!

[TREVOR *groans.* STANLEY *nods and switches off the cellar light. He switches the main light on.*]

STANLEY: That's what he's done. Trod on a frog. He's not dead. Only stunned. Cover yourself up, Mother. Mum? Cover yourself, Mum. For pity's sake.

[*He holds her dressing-gown up for her. She stares at him, and cries.*]

[*FAST BLACKOUT.*]

[*SOUND ONLY. Two ambulance men are with* STANLEY *and* TREVOR. *There is the sound of an ambulance klaxon. A door bangs. The klaxon stops.*]

ONE: Eee. He's a pretty picture i'n't he?

TWO: What's his name?

STANLEY: Trevor.

TWO: Aye . . the question is, did he jump, or was he pushed?

STANLEY: No . . . he trod on a frog, you see.

ONE: Oooh dear, poor sod.

STANLEY: Who?

ONE: Him.

STANLEY: Oh, oh yeah, but you should see the frog. Flattened it he did. It must have struggled all the way up to that top step, in the dark, just stopped for a breather, and then . . . [*squelching noise*] It's no kind of life, really, is it?

TWO: Yes, well, what we'll do . . . we'll check the

damage first, and then, Trevor, what I want you to do, I want you to tell me the minute you feel anything – right?

[TREVOR *groans.*]

Now, Trev, how about this leg?

[TREVOR *screams.*]

I see. How about this one then?

[TREVOR *screams.*]

Right, well. You won't be playing football for a bit then.

STANLEY: I told him, you know. I said: 'Always watch out when frogs are about'. But he never listened.

TWO: What about this arm then, Trev?

[TREVOR *screams.*]

Oh. I suppose the other one's much the same, but . . .

[TREVOR *screams.*]

Yeah. Thought so. Now then, Trev. I'm going to put you in the picture. We're going to have to carry you up these steps. So . . . if it hurts at all, well, you just tell us, OK? I mean, you don't have to scream right in our ears, you know. Just say: 'That hurts a bit' . . . and we'll stop for a rest. OK? Yeah.

[TREVOR *groans.*]

Right then, and a one, and a two and an altogether now!

[*LIGHTS UP.*]

Scene Eleven

Hospital. A small two-bed room. One bed, hidden by a screen, contains SHANE PRITCHARD. *In the second bed is* TREVOR, *spread-eagled by ropes and pulleys, his legs protected by a cage under the sheet. Both arms and both legs are broken, and in plaster. He's bandaged round the ribs, round his head, and has a plaster across his nose.* SGT HARRY ASQUITH *stands with one foot on a bedside chair, munching grapes, discreetly spitting the pips under* SHANE*'s bed.* SHANE *sings to himself but with great vehemence.*

SHANE: 'If I ruled the world
Every man would have his
Da da dee da
If I ruled the world!'

[*Silence.*]

HARRY: Still, you know, Trevor, it could have been worse. It could have been worse. It's hard to see how, but . . .

[TREVOR *groans.*]

SHANE: 'If I ruled the world
Every man would get his
Da dee dee dum
Every da would get his
Da da dee dum
If I ruled the world!'

[*Silence.* HARRY*'s about to speak when* SHANE *starts singing again.*]

'I!
I who have nothing
I!
I who have no-one.'

[HARRY *waits for more then moves the chair nearer* TREVOR. *Silence.*]

HARRY: Is, er, is he all right?

TREVOR: He's had a bollock off.

HARRY: Oh, well then . . .

SHANE: 'If I ruled the world
Every da would get his
Da da dee da!
Every man would get his
Dee dee di dum!
If I ruled the world!'

[*Pause.*]

HARRY: Did it, er, did it just work loose, or . . .?

TREVOR: He were a driving instructor. Emergency stop. Crushed it in the gear stick. Had to have it off.

HARRY: Ooooo dear.

SHANE: I'm not deaf! I know you're talking about me.

TREVOR: I was just telling him, about your bollock.

SHANE: I'll kill you! Shut up! I'll kill you!

HARRY: No, no, mum's the word with me cock. Don't fret. And, there again, it could have been worse, couldn't it? You don't really *need* two. Even with one, you've got enough stuff to cover the Isle of Man twice over. Seen it on the telly! And, it doesn't affect your balance or anything. It doesn't make you go bald or anything.

TREVOR: It just looks a bit funny.

SHANE: I'll kill you; shut up!

HARRY: No, no, I mean, I wouldn't like it to happen to me. Given the choice. But . . . it could have been worse. You've got to look on the bright side, haven't you? What you do, switch the light off before you get undressed. Nobody'll be any the wiser. And, if you go swimming, just shove an egg down your trunks. But, hard-boiled, or pot. Not fresh. [*to* TREVOR] We have automatics now, on the Pandas.

[TREVOR *groans.*]

Oh, I know how you feel, Trev.

TREVOR: Oh no you don't.

HARRY: Oh yes I do. Believe me I do. I was in here you know. For haemorrhoids. That's no joke. And I know what happened, you know; I know everything that happened. You don't have to tell me a thing. Unless you want to. [*pause*] Right now. Listen. I've been married five times as long as you. Nearly ten years. Ten. The point is, if I can put up with what I get, why can't you? I make do. I do. And what about Irene? How do you think she's feeling at this precise moment in time?

[*There is a knock at the door.* IRENE *puts her head round the door.*]

IRENE: Can I come in?

HARRY: Irene! Come in, come in. I've just been giving him a few 'words of wisdom'. You've had your hair done!

[IRENE *flashes him an 'oh, you noticed' smile.*]

IRENE: Hello, Trev.

TREVOR: Er, hello.

[SHIRLEY *and* ERIC *enter, with flowers.*]

SHIRLEY: Hello, Trev.

TREVOR: Er . . .

ERIC: Hello, Trev.

TREVOR: Oh.

[*They laugh and gather round him.* IRENE *flashes* HARRY *a big smile.*]

HARRY: I told him what it'd come to. Treading on a frog at his age. Yeah. Well, er . . .

[IRENE *straightens his tie, gives him a kiss, and pats his cheeks.*]

IRENE: Don't frown, Harry. Don't fret, pet.

HARRY: Oh.

IRENE: 'Bye, 'bye.

HARRY: Oh.

[SHIRLEY *giggles.*]

Right, upstairs. We'll see if Mrs Baldry's laughing, eh?

[HARRY *leaves, not happily.* SHIRLEY *giggles.*]

IRENE: Trev? Everything's going to be *all right,* Trev.

TREVOR: I can't . . . talk . . . much. I trod . . . on a frog. It hurts.

IRENE: Yes, yes. Now just let me tell you what's happened to me. Well . . . it started when I stopped taking the pills. Sedatives. My mind was all in a whirl and I was sitting still, trying to think, but . . . Mum just wouldn't shurrup. Yackety-clacking away she were, and telling me what I should do, and what I shouldn't do, and . . . Dad were just sitting there, in his chair, looking so sad and cracking his knuckles, and sighing and, I just felt . . . I've got to get away from all of this! So, I did. I left. Walked out. But I didn't know where to go. So I walked down to the shop, and I stood there, staring at it. But, I didn't want to be alone, in an empty house. I'd left Glenda with my mum. I didn't know where to go. I didn't have anywhere I could go. So, I went on walking. And it come on raining, and dark, and cold, and I walked right up to the Reservoir and back down Longbottom Wood, back to the shop again and . . . and then . . .

it come on me like a streak of lightning, Trevor! Like a voice inside me, urging me on. 'Eric and Shirley! Eric and Shirley! Shirley and Eric!' Like a magnet, pulling me. So, I knocked on the door, and it opened, and inside it were all bright and warm, and they were smiling so warmly and Eric just said, ever so soft, he said: 'Come inside, Irene love'. And I just broke down. Something inside just . . . snapped. I were shivering, and crying . . . shaking! I could not stop crying, Trev! I couldn't!

SHIRLEY: Sobbing her socks off.

ERIC: Frightened hell out of the cat.

[SHIRLEY *giggles.*]

IRENE: I felt just so absolutely alone, Trev. I felt like I'd been alone for so long. So lost. And I was trying to explain, between crying, and . . . oh dear. It was like having flu. But then, this wonderful thing happened. Shirley and Eric just got down on the floor with me. I was all huddled up, on the rug, *you know*, and . . . they cuddled me! And it was just what I needed! Just the very thing. A good cuddle.

[*She wipes away the tears, smiling.* ERIC *and* SHIRLEY *hold hands.*]

And then, well, I just said it! Me! I said: '*Please*, can we take our clothes off?' And Eric said: 'Oh, all right'. So we did. And then we cuddled again. We cuddled and cuddled, and hugged, and stroked, and . . . oh, it was so warm, Trev. So safe. It was like being the filling in a sandwich. Lovely. And then I said: 'Shall we go to bed?' So we did. We went upstairs, still cuddling, and we all had a hot bath together and dried each other off and . . .

and then we went to bed. And it was *sublime*! A wonderful, beautiful, night.

TREVOR: You . . . you mean . . . you . . . and Eric?

IRENE: Oh, me and Eric, and Shirley and Eric, and Shirley and me *and* Eric. Oh, it was gorgeous! Oh, Trevor, I do wish you could have been with us.

SHIRLEY: Never mind. There's plenty of time. Eh, Trev?

IRENE: There's all our lives! Oh, I've never been so wonderfully tired out in all my life. It was so . . . *warm*, Trev. And, you know what, Trev? You know what?

SHANE: What? What?

IRENE: I did everything! I did! I did! Everything. Shirley showed me how, and then I had a go, and Eric went just wild, and, oh, Trevor, I don't give a toss about germs and microbes. I like it! It feels lovely. And, Eric says, with a bit more practice I'll get better and better at it, didn't you, Eric?

ERIC: She's very good. Really.

IRENE: So, you see, Trev, there's *nothing* wrong *any more*! Everything is wonderful. Fucking, and sucking, and licking, and squeezing . . . I think it's beautiful! It is, i'n't it, Trev? I'n't it beautiful?

TREVOR: Er . . .

IRENE: And, you know, you were quite right. It's not just sex. It's love! I can love you, and Glenda, *and* Eric *and* Shirley and . . . everybody, anybody else who wants to love me!

SHANE: Er . . . excuse me.

IRENE: Oh, Trevor!

[*She hugs him.*]

TREVOR: AAAARGH! My ribs! My ribs!

IRENE: What's up, love, are you not happy?

TREVOR: Yes, but . . . it hurts!

[*There is a knock at the door.* HARRY *enters.*]

HARRY: I thought you might like to know that they're going to let Mrs Baldry go home tomorrow. Cleared her rash right up. Perfume caused it. Something or other d'Amour. Cheap but smelly. But they don't think she can keep on looking after Stanley, what with him being missing a slate. They're going to keep him where he is. In the Home. She's signed the papers. He's committed. Well, bit big to have under your feet, after all. Like puppies after Christmas, i'n't it? They won't stop growing, so . . . still he'll get used to it. I mean, you get used to anything if you have to, don't you? Well, you don't, but well . . . tarra then.

[*He leaves.* TREVOR *groans.*]

SHIRLEY: [*rising*] Oh, come on, Trev. Let's think about something else, eh?

[*She tidies his sheets.*]

Irene?

IRENE: Mm?

SHIRLEY: [*lifting the sheet*] About the only thing he didn't break, eh?

IRENE: Oh, Godfrey. We call it Godfrey, after his Uncle, don't we, Trev?

TREVOR: Er, now and again, now and again . . .

SHIRLEY: Eric, tell Trevor about . . . you know. The plan.

ERIC: Oh. Yeah. Well, you know, ah, Trev . . . we got to talking a bit, after . . . when we woke up.

IRENE: Ooo, isn't he handsome? Oh, Godfrey . . .

ERIC: I mean, we reckoned you'd probably had just about enough of shopkeeping.

TREVOR: Mmmm?

ERIC: Yeah. And, well, I'm not getting a *lot* of satisfaction out of selling secondhand cars.

IRENE: Shall I?

SHIRLEY: Be a devil.

[IRENE *looks for somewhere to hang her handbag. She hooks it over* TREVOR*'s hand.*]

ERIC: So, we got to thinking about other ways of life. New ways.

TREVOR: Oh.

[IRENE *ducks under the sheet.*]

Oh! Mmm . . .

ERIC: Yeah, and, I said I'd always had a bit of a yearning for something a bit closer to nature. Something . . . earthy.

TREVOR: Mmm . . . Oooo . . .

ERIC: Yeah. So Irene said: 'Well, farming's earthy'. And I thought: 'She's quite right!'

TREVOR: Yes! Yes!

ERIC: Yeah. So, first off, we thought about crops. Tilling, ploughing . . . and that . . .

SHANE: Arable.

ERIC: Yeah. But then I thought: 'Well, what with tractors and combine-harvesters and all the tackle, it'll be a bit like a garage all over again'.

TREVOR: Uh?

ERIC: No, it would. So then we thought about cows. But they seemed a bit big.

TREVOR: Mmmm! Oh.

ERIC: So then we thought about pigs for a bit. But they are very sloppy, really.

TREVOR: Groooo . . .

ERIC: And well, I don't like sheep. So that left us with fowls. Hens.

TREVOR: Ah! Mmm . . .

ERIC: Yeah. They're small, they're pretty-looking, and they're quite friendly. They do peck a bit, but not in cages. Batteries, you know. You just put the grub in one end and pull the eggs out the other. And then, when they stop laying, you knock them on the head, shove them through a mechanical plucker, plastic bags, in the deep freeze, and there you are: farmyard fresh chickens.

[SHIRLEY *has been munching the chocolates bought for* TREVOR. *She offers him one. He shakes his head.*]

TREVOR: Uh-uh. Oh! Oy! Uuuu . . .

ERIC: Oh, and we thought we'd call ourselves *SHIRLENE Poultry Products.* That's Shirley and Irene put together. Do you get it?

TREVOR: Yes! Yes!

ERIC: Yeah. So, ah, what do you say, Trev?

TREVOR: Ooooh, yes, yes. YES. YES! YE-E-ES . . .

ERIC: Oh good. But you do really think we could make a go of it, do you?

TREVOR: Oh yes, yes, oh. You've talked me into it.

SHANE: Er, I know a thing or two about chickens, you know. I do. Hello? Cock-a-doodle-doo? I do, though, I do.

[*They all laugh.*]

TREVOR: Oooh, it does hurt when I laugh. It hurts! It hurts!

[*They all laugh as music comes in* – 'It Was Just One of Those Things'.]

[*THE LIGHTS FADE AND THE CURTAIN FALLS.*]

THE END